YOUTUBE COOKBOOK

Secrets to Your Channel's Success

ODIEN ANOMA

*This book is dedicated to my family, for being
a source of encouragement to me.*

CONTENTS

INTRODUCTION

YouTube, an American online video sharing platform owned by Google, is the second most visited website after Google search.

So many Youtubers have made a living just by posting videos and receiving their income via this platform.

By starting a YouTube channel, you have to consider it as a business.

The two main things to consider before starting your channel is Time and Budget.

If after considering these two main factors and you are ready. Follow through with me as I show you proven tips to grow your channel as a beginner or boost your channel as a current YouTuber.

CHAPTER 1
HOW DO I START?

All you need to start your channel is to pick a particular **NICHE**, one that you are sure will keep you **consistent** in creating **quality** videos.

It could be Technology, Finance, Gaming, Tutorials, Vlogs, Food, Fitness, Fashion, Humor, etc.

Make sure to pick just **ONE** niche for your channel. This makes the work easier and drives your target audience faster.

CHAPTER 2
HOW TO CUSTOMIZE YOUR CHANNEL NAME AND DESCRIPTION
[THE RIGHT WAY]

1. First, decide on a unique name that no other YouTube channel uses, as the name for your YouTube Channel.

2. In your channel description, you can write brief story of yourself, who you are, what you are about, why they should subscribe and what you want them to do.

FORMAT:

"Welcome to .... YouTube Channel.

My name is...... I am a...... When you Subscribe to my channel you are going to get ... value. Every single week, I upload a video or more for you. Please Subscribe today and turn on the Notification by hitting the bell."

3. Make sure to add your e-mail address in there for Sponsorships, Partnerships or Promotions as well as the link to your channel.

FORMAT:

For Sponsorship and Promotion, Contact me at (E-mail address)

My YouTube Channel: (Channel Link)

CHAPTER 3

CREATING HIGH-RANKING VIDEOS

Creating videos to be in line with YouTube Algorithm and gain more Subscribers can be achieved in no time by implementing what I will be showing you.

The following tips will be your guide.

GET YOUR KEYWORDS READY:

1. Use Keyword research tools to find keywords for your videos. I recommend Google Trends, Ahrefs or SEMrush.

2. Use keywords that has low competition most times.

CHAPTER 4
YOUTUBE VIDEO MAKING TIPS

1. Make sure the aspect ratio for your video is 16:9 (YouTube Standard Aspect Ratio) and your video dimension is 1920px by 1080px (YouTube Standard Video Dimension).

NOTE: This doesn't mean that if your video dimension or aspect ratio is not according to YouTube standard it won't be uploaded.

2. Use animations, animation texts, movie scene, YouTube clips, or you as the youtuber talking, interchangeably in your videos.

When using movie scene make sure it's in line with **Fair Use Policy.**

TIPS ON USING MOVIE SCENE:
- ➤ Do not use the entire video instead use clips and add some transformation like audios, reactions, etc.

- ➤ The scene shouldn't affect the commercial success of the real video owner.

- ➤ Use free footage from Pexels, Pixabay or playphrase.me to avoid copyright claims.

3. When beginning a video (mostly educative videos), you can start with a story having a prologue format like, "Come on a journey with me...". Then,

    - Tell the story with a blend of both information and entertainment. It must be emotional, either positively or negatively and you can do this with a blend of music and video clips.

- Put the problem forward.

- Get the audience amped up by making the video relatable. A format to use is "And then there's you..." to make the video engaging.

- Finally, get to the solution.

4. In your video, say the exact keywords like five times to help YouTube algorithm push the video to your target audience.

5. Your video should give a different perspective or re-affirm an existing perspective to your audience after watching. They should be like **"I need more"**.

6. Make sure to tell your viewers to subscribe, like, share and comment below. **NEVER** assume they know it.

FORMAT:
"Hey, if this is your first time watching my video or visiting my channel, make sure to hit the Subscribe button, Like and Share."

- You can say it at the beginning, middle or end of your videos. Do this interchangeably in your different videos.

7. Be **consistent** on uploading **quality** videos.

CHAPTER 5

CREATING A FACELESS YOUTUBE CHANNEL

So many YouTubers have exceeded amazingly by creating faceless YouTube video. The following steps would guide you in creating faceless YouTube videos.

STEPS TO CREATE A FACELESS YOUTUBE VIDEO:

1. Your videos should follow the **YOUTUBE VIDEOS MAKING TIPS** above.

2. Write down your script. An easy way to write your script is by visiting **Copy.ai**. This site will automatically write the scripts for you after putting your descriptions and keywords. Otherwise, you can write it yourself or pay a freelancer on **Fiverr** to do it for you.

3. Make a voice-over for your script either by recording your voice as you read the script, pay a freelancer on **Fiverr** or you use a Text to Speech Converter software. I recommend **Balabolka** for your Personal Computer or **Narrator's voice - TTS** for mobile phones.

4. After creating your audio recording, go to **Pexels** to get free videos to match the message of your video. You can use the **Audio Library** in your YouTube Studio, to get free audios and music for your content without any copyright claims.

5. Synchronize both the audio and video together. I recommend using **VSDC Video Editor** for Personal

Computers or **Video Editor – Video.Guru** for mobile phones.

6. Make sure your video's file name matches the title of your video when uploading to YouTube.

CHAPTER 6
YOUTUBE SHORTS [SIMPLIFIED]

This is a short-form video-sharing platform. Its's YouTube's version of TikTok and the following tips would help you get started and ready for monetization in no time.

TIPS TO UPLOAD SHORTS:

1. The time frame for your shorts should be sixty seconds or less. The lesser the better.
2. Dimension of **1080px by 1920px.**
3. Shorts layout should be **vertical**.
4. Aspect ratio of **9:10.**
5. Create your video.
6. Remind viewers to subscribe or add a Subscribe button GIF to the end of your video.
7. Add subtitles to your video.
8. Follow the **TIPS ON CREATING VIDEO TITLE** above.
9. Always use **"#shorts"** tag after your video title.
10. You can add two more keywords that relates to your video as tags. Example: #shorts, **#calisthenics, #workout**. Follow **GUIDELINE TO WRITING TAGS** below.

❖ I recommend using **VSDC Video Editor** for Personal Computers or **Video Editor – Video.Guru** for mobile phones to edit your shorts videos.

❖ Tutorials on how to use any of the video editors can be found on YouTube.

NOTE: For your video to upload as a **SHORTS** video, you **MUST**

follow the **time frame, dimension, layout** and **aspect ratio** above.

CHAPTER 7

GUIDELINE TO WRITING TAGS

Tags like **#shorts, #viral**, and so on are written in the same box you write your title name. The also help YouTube understand what kind of video you make and rank it higher.

Where do you position your tags?

You position your tags to the right after the title name of your video. The recommended maximum number for your tags should be **three**.

TAGS CHECKLIST:
1. Main Keyword: (Sit-up)
2. Variations: (Workout)
3. Category: (Fitness)

Example: **How to Do a Perfect Sit-up (5 EASY STEPS) #situp #workout #fitness**

Title (required) ⑦
How to Do a Perfect Sit-up (5 EASY STEPS) #shorts #workout #fitness

CHAPTER 8
CREATING A COMPELLING VIDEO TITLE THAT HOOKS ANYONE

1. You need a compelling title that hooks your audience. Example:
   - **How To...**
   - **How I...**
   - **Secrets Of...**
   - **5 Secrets To ...**
   - **Don't Start ... Until You Watch This**
   - **Top 7 Most Dangerous Creatures**

2. Your title must be less than fifty-five characters and between ten to thirty words.

3. Add an emoji to make the algorithm understand your videos more and push it to a wider audience.

4. Your Title must contain your Keyword.

5. Use parenthesis and brackets. **Example: How to Grow Your YouTube Subscribers (NEW METHOD REVEALED)**

6. Use numbers like years, number of steps or tips, amount. Using decimal numbers as well as odd numbers will give you a boost. **Example: 7 Tips to earn over $3,788.85/month in Affiliate Marketing.**

7. After your title name, include at most three tags. Follow **GUIDELINE TO WRITING TAGS** above.

12

CHAPTER 9

WRITING YOUR VIDEO DESCRIPTION ACCURATELY

- Focus on the first two to three sentences on your description. Most times, the first word should be your Keyword.

- Do not include links in the beginning of your description.

- Description must start with the benefits viewers will gain. This is because viewers tend to see the first sentence of your video description and decide whether to watch or not.

- Repeat your main keywords two to three times in your whole description.

- Use related keywords in your video description. Example, if your main keyword is Sit-up or Calisthenics, you can use related keywords like gym, workout, fitness, etc.

- Learn from the keywords in your competitor's videos.

- Description should be conversational.

- The higher the number of words in your video description, the higher it will rank. You can use half your original video subtitles as your description.

- After your video description, you tell them to Subscribe in the description box and then you can finally add your links (if any) there.

CHAPTER 10
DESIGNING EYE-CATCHING THUMBNAILS

Your thumbnail is one of the first things, viewers see when YouTube shows your video. Hence, it **MUST** stand out.

THUMBNAIL CHECKLIST:

➢ Use mostly colors like **Blue, Orange, Green** and **Yellow**. These colors help your videos thumbnails to stand out from YouTube main colors which are Red, Black and White.
NOTE: This doesn't mean you can't add a touch of Red, Black or White to your thumbnails. The goal is to make them eye-catching.

➢ Most YouTubers use pictures of celebrities as part of their thumbnail to make it stand out.

CHAPTER 11
WHEN TO UPLOAD YOUR VIDEOS

Knowing the days and time to post on YouTube will help boost your view, as this is the best time, your viewers will be active on the platform.

DAYS AND TIME TO POST:

- **MONDAYS: 2PM TO 4PM**
- **TUESDAYS: 2PM TO 4PM**
- **WEDNESDAYS: 2PM TO 4PM**
- **THURSDAYS: 12PM TO 3PM**
- **FRIDAYS: 12PM TO 3PM**
- **SATURDAYS: 9AM TO 11AM**
- **SUNDAYS: 9AM TO 11AM**

NOTE:

1. **Mondays, Tuesdays and Wednesdays are not really good days. But if you feel you should upload your video, then go ahead.**

2. **Fridays, Saturdays, and Sundays are the PEAK days to upload your videos.**

3. **You may also have to tweak the times you upload your videos to study your audience.**

CHAPTER 12

THE UPLOADING PROCESS

This process starts when you click the **UPLOAD** button on your YouTube Studio.

1. Follow **TIPS ON CREATING VIDEO TITLE** above.

2. Follow **GUIDELINE TO WRITING TAGS** above.

3. Follow **TIPS ON WRITING VIDEO DESCRIPTION** above.

4. Follow **YOUTUBE THUMBNAILS GUIDE** above.

5. Always upload a transcript or subtitle for your video. This helps to rank your videos not just on YouTube but also on Google.

6. Make sure to add End Screens during your upload process. End Screens are thumbnails overlays which encourages viewers to click on another video of yours, subscribe to your channel, etc.

➤ You can find tutorials on how to add end screens to your videos on YouTube

7. Add Cards to your videos. Cards helps you share clickable links to content during the course of your video. The maximum number of cards you can add is **five**.

- **Video or Playlist Card** to promote your video.
- **Link Card** to link an approved website off of YouTube

- **Channel Card** to promote your channel or another YouTube channel
- **Donation Card** to feature a non-profit event or any event of your choice and spur on donations
- **Poll Card** to encourage your viewers to engage in multi-choice question polls.

➤ You can find tutorials on how to add cards to your videos on YouTube

8. Promote your best videos in playlist by putting them in categories. Example, let's say you have a Fitness Channel you can divide the playlists into Push Up Playlist, Calisthenics Playlist, Arm Workout Playlist, etc.

CHAPTER 13
ENGAGING YOUR AUDIENCE

The more you engage with your audience and subscribers. The more they stay subscribed to your channel. The following tips would help you do that.

1. Make sure to fall in love with your fans and subscribers as you do with your content.

2. Ask them what they would want you to upload in your next video.

3. Interact with your fans in the comments sections, pin some of their comments and also give a heart reaction to it.

4. Engage with fans in community posts by giving them a sneak peek of your next video or asking multiple choice questions. The more they respond, the more YouTube ranks your videos.

5. Do Giveaways.

6. Upload **quality** and **consistent** content.

CHAPTER 14
FREE TRAFFIC TO YOUR YOUTUBE CHANNEL

1. **Blogs**: You can create your website and write articles on that niche then post your YouTube video link.

If you don't have a website, you can guest blog on other people's blog sites or simply use **Medium.com**

2. **TikTok**: You can create a TikTok channel for that particular niche and make short videos. Make sure to add your YouTube link when editing your TikTok bio.

3. **Social Media Platforms (Facebook, WhatsApp, Instagram, Twitter, etc.)**: Post teaser clips and links to your video.

4. **Comments:** Comment exclusively on other YouTube channels (mostly related channels) and invite them to check out your channel.

5. **Pinterest**

6. **LinkedIn**

7. **Quora**

8. **Reddit**

9. **Forums**

10. **Slideshare.net**

11. **E-mails**

12. **Friends of Friends (Recommendation)**

Etc.

CHAPTER 15
SIX WAYS TO EARN PASSIVE INCOME FROM YOUR CHANNEL

1. Ads revenue

2. Sponsorship and Promotions

3. Crowdfunding

4. Channel Memberships

5. Selling Personal products and

6. Affiliate marketing.

NOTE: ALWAYS add a disclaimer on your YouTube description, when promoting a product as an affiliate.

Here's a format,

 "We may receive a commission when you click the link and make a purchase, without any additional cost occurring to you".

CHAPTER 16

KEY

TO YOUR CHANNEL SUCCESS

You should consider your YouTube channel as a **long-term business** and the **key** to succeeding in this business is by being **consistent** and uploading **quality** content.

www.ingramcontent.com/pod-product-compliance
Lightning Source LLC
Chambersburg PA
CBHW051407250726
48656CB00006B/2318